MEHMET
THE CONQUEROR

Written by
EMMA CLARK
&
Illustrated by
LAURA DE LA MARE

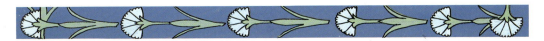

Copyright © Hood Hood Books 1998

Hood Hood Books
46 Clabon Mews
London SW1X OEH
Tel: 44.171.5847878
Fax: 44.171.2250386

British Library Cataloguing–in–Publication Data
A catalogue record for this book is available from the British Library

ISBN 1 900251 17 5

Origination by Fine Line Graphics - London.
Printed by IPH, Egypt.

MEHMET

IT WAS A CLEAR AND STARRY NIGHT IN THE LATE SPRING OF 1453 and a Venetian ship was anchored in the Mediterranean sea near the Turkish coast. As it bobbed gently on the waves a somewhat plump fellow with a friendly face and a dark beard could be seen pacing carefully up and down the deck. His name was Niccolo Barbaro. He was the ship's doctor and he had eaten rather too much for dinner. "Oh dear," he sighed as he looked up at the moon and the stars, "it really is rather beautiful tonight – if only I hadn't...." Suddenly, he stood still, and craning his neck

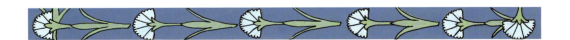

upwards, he rubbed his eyes instead of his stomach. "Hello, what's this? I'm sure it's supposed to be a full moon tonight; the captain was just talking to me about it at dinner." His mind cleared. "Yes, it should definitely be a full moon and I'm looking at a new moon, probably only three days old. Oh no, what does this mean?" Deep down, with great foreboding the ship's doctor knew exactly what this meant. With a grave look on his face he went to fetch the captain to show him the new moon which should have been a full moon.

The whole ship's crew came up on deck to look at the new moon. It stayed like that for four whole hours and they all knew that this could only signify one thing: the fall of Constantinople. It had been foretold that when the moon was a strange shape then this "Queen of Cities", capital of the East Roman Empire since its foundation by Constantine the Great in 324 A.D., would fall to the Turks. For over a thousand years this great city had been ruled without interruption by ninety-two emperors. However, this was before Mehmet (Turkish for Muhammad) II appeared, a fearless young man with the

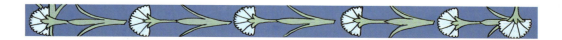

heart of a tiger and the brilliance of an experienced general.

Mehmet II was born in 1432 in Edirne and from the beginning was a rebellious child, determined to get his own way. He outwitted one tutor after another until at last his father found someone really tough called Mollah Gurani. In the first lesson, Mehmet refused to take any notice of him, as was usual. However, unlike the other tutors, who pleaded pathetically, "oh, please behave Your Royal Highness, please try and learn some Arabic verbs today," he just picked up the biggest ruler Mehmet had ever seen and, waving it menacingly in the air, roared, "this is to make you obey – so get to work!" The young prince was very impressed by this method and from that day on he studied hard and learnt very fast. He learnt Turkish, Persian, Arabic and probably Greek and Serbo-Croat as well. He learnt to recite the whole Quran by heart and read much Persian literature too.

Clearly very intelligent, Mehmet was also ambitious and determined, and from a young age he threw himself into the study of warfare. His role-model was the Greek hero and conqueror, Alexander the Great. In fact he used to make one of his servants

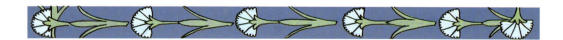

read out loud to him from the life of Alexander every day. By the age of twenty, when Mehmet heard the news of his father's death, instead of bursting into tears as most dutiful sons did, he leapt onto his favourite Arab horse and shouted, "Let those who love me, follow me!"

So, in 1451, Mehmet was at last on the Ottoman throne. However, he was not exactly safe and secure. His father's death had caused much instability at home and this made the Empire look weak in the eyes of its enemies – who were quick to take advantage. Mehmet realised how vital it was to have one strong leader and knew he had to be ruthless for the safety and strength of the realm. So, shortly after becoming Sultan he had his younger brother killed and then passed a new law making it legal for Sultans to kill their brothers! It was not unusual in those days for brother to turn against brother or son against father. Mehmet's law held good for about two hundred years. After that the Sultan's brothers were no longer killed but were imprisoned in the Royal Palace in what came to be known as the "Gilded Cage" – but that is another story.

As soon as he became Sultan, Mehmet started preparing for the capture of the greatest goal of his forefathers – Constantinople. He collected his best troops from all over the Empire. These were known as the Janisseries (from the Turkish *Yeni Ceri* meaning "New Soldiers"), famous for their courage in warfare and their highly disciplined and religious way of life. He constructed a fortress on the Bosphorous called Rumeli Hisar where he built up the most technologically advanced weapons the world had ever seen: artillery, bombardments and a monster-size cannon with a barrel twenty-five feet long which could fire a quarter-ton stone cannon-ball for over a mile – a tremendous feat in those days.

At last, in the late Spring of 1453, Mehmet II was ready for his assault on Constantinople. His brave and dedicated soldiers

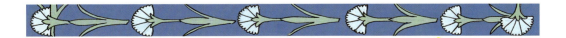

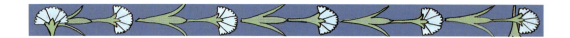

launched themselves at the city walls; but Constantine XI, the last Byzantine Emperor, and his small army would not give up without a fight. In spite of much bloodshed, Mehmet could not capture the fortress-like city on foot. The only way to break through was to sail his ships into the Golden Horn, the natural harbour of the city – but how could he do this? The harbour had a massive chain hanging across its entrance, blocking it off to all enemy ships. Mehmet thought quickly and came up with a most ingenious plan. He announced to his astonished generals and captains that if they could not sail their ships into the Golden Horn, they would simply take them overland!

First of all he ordered hundreds of trees to be cut down and sawn into planks. The planks of wood were heavily greased with sheep's fat and laid side by side to cover the whole hill between the Bosphorous and the Golden Horn. Then he gathered together dozens of the strongest oxen he could find and lashed them to seventy of his ships. They pulled and dragged and heaved the ships up and over the hill and into the waters of the Golden Horn. The ships unfurled their sails so it really looked like they were

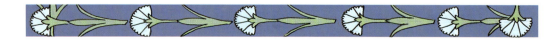

sailing overland! Imagine the shock of the poor inhabitants of the city when they woke up to find the enemy ships bobbing about right under their noses!

Mehmet's soldiers could now attack from all sides and eventually, after weeks of fierce and desperate fighting, the emperor and inhabitants were forced to surrender their beloved city. In Western Europe the fall of Constantinople was "the darkest day in the history of the world". To the Ottomans, of course, it was quite the opposite!

On Easter Monday, 29th May 1453, Sultan Mehmet II rode on his white horse into the famous city of Constantinople. He had achieved his greatest prize at only twenty-one years old and has been known ever since as "Fatih", Turkish for "Conqueror." His very first act on entering the city was to approach the great cathedral of Haghia Sophia (meaning Holy Wisdom) built by the Emperor Justinian 900 years earlier, dismount, and bend down and touch his forehead on the ground in an act of gratitude and submission before God.

From that time on Constantinople was Constantinople no

longer: Mehmet renamed it Istanbul, and the cathedral of Haghia Sophia became the mosque of Aya Sofya. The city had declined in recent years and Mehmet now set about restoring it to its former glory and his first act was to repopulate it. He brought in people from all over the empire – different nationalities and different religions. In fact by the time of his great-grandson, Suleiman the Magnificent, it was estimated that there were seventy-two and a half nationalities living together in Istanbul – the half being the gypsies because they never stayed in one place long enough! He determined to make it a capital fit for the "Sultan of the Two Continents", "Emperor of the Two Seas" and "Favourite of God on the Two Horizons" as he called himself. He put to work the many Greek, Armenian, Turkish and Italian artisans and craftsmen who had recently moved to the city, commissioning them to build houses, mosques, baths, inns, market-places and workshops, as well as restoring roads, aqueducts and sewers. The new building programme included a mosque named after himself, the "Fatih Mosque", with a large dome to rival the Haghia Sophia.

At the same time Mehmet thought hard about where to house his seat of government and also where to build a truly splendid palace to live in. He now called a whole train of viziers and servants and prepared to roam the city to find the most spectacular position on which to build a worthy palace.

It was not hard to find. Mehmet chose Seraglio Point, a piece of land jutting out with a wonderful view overlooking all three seas: the Sea of Marmara, the Bosphorous and the Golden Horn. In 1459 he started the building of the Topkapi Saray (meaning Cannon Gate Palace), a palace that he wanted to outshine all preceding palaces in looks, size, cost and gracefulness. It really was magnificent, a city within a city where as many as fifty thousand people could live. It came to be known as the "Abode of Felicity" and included the great room where the affairs of state were discussed. This was called the Imperial *Divan* and the Sultan had a special room where he could sit and listen to what was going on without being seen. At first, he used to sit with his viziers in the *Divan* itself but one day a messenger burst in and asked: "Which of you is the fortunate sovereign?" Mehmet, the

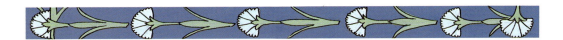

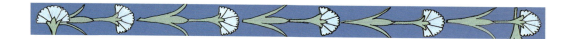

"Sultan of the Two Seas", was angry at not being instantly recognised and thereafter attended the *Divan* from his special hidden room – "behind the curtain" as it came to be known.

At the heart of the Topkapi Palace were the private apartments, known as the "Harem" (meaning forbidden place) where his wife, children and other ladies of the court lived, along with their servants. In fact no other men were allowed here at all: those who came to deliver firewood were called the "firemen with lovelocks" because they were ordered to grow their hair with specially long curls so that they could not glimpse the women!

Mehmet not only enjoyed building his new palace, which was finished in 1478, but was also passionate about gardening. In the courtyards and gardens at the Topkapi Palace hundreds of gardeners were employed to take care of the flowers, plants, fruit-trees and vegetables, as well as birds and animals. Peacocks strutted majestically and gazelles roamed gracefully amongst the trees and fountains; Mehmet would listen to the water gently trickling in the streams and pools while delighting in the scent of the roses and reading Persian poetry.

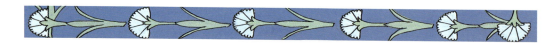

Under him Istanbul flourished with many cultures, customs and religions mixing together. Unlike his ancestors, who were basically warriors who felt much more at home with a sword in their hand than a book, Mehmet II was cultured and well-educated. He was genuinely interested in encouraging learning – including the study of religion, philosophy and the sciences – in his new-found capital, wanting to be remembered as a philosopher-king as well as a warrior. He brought scholars into the city, established schools known as *madrasa*s and was very tolerant of other religions, allowing Christians and Jews to worship freely.

As well as having religious, cultural and literary interests Mehmet was a master at managing the affairs of his ever-growing empire. He issued a new law-book (known as the *kanunname* or "Code of the Conquerors") which regulated every tiny detail of life for everyone in the city, right down to the colour of the clothes worn. The members of every rank, from humble page-boy to Grand Vizier, knew not only the tasks they had to perform, but also what clothes they should wear and how long their beards should grow. For example, the viziers wore green turbans, the

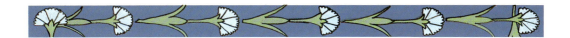

Muslim religious leaders, called the *ulema*, wore purple and the master of the horse was dressed from head to toe in dark green.

However, Mehmet did not spend as much time as he would have liked in his flourishing capital city and in his gardens. In fact most of his time was taken up in planning campaigns and reminding his enemies that he was not called the "Sultan of the Two Continents" for nothing. The problem was that after the big prize of Istanbul, all other conquests were really small-fry to Mehmet. "It's a bit like eating the main course before the starter", he observed one day rather sadly to his Grand Vizier: "where shall we go next?" His Grand Vizier replied, "Padishah" (meaning "Great King" in Persian), "why not go further west into Europe?" knowing full well that this was what Mehmet intended. For there was one prize that was even greater than Constantinople and that was the ultimate prize of all – Rome.

However, as great a military genius as Mehmet was, this was beyond his grasp. He had to content himself with conquering Bosnia and Serbia, followed by Greece, Albania and the Crimea. He certainly lived up to his title of the "Conqueror!"

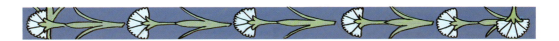

Mehmet died in May 1481, at only forty-eight years old. He had many enemies both at home and abroad – the rulers of Venice, for instance, tried to poison him fourteen times. However, it was probably his own son Bayezid II, who finally had him poisoned, and who became the next, eighth, Sultan of the Ottoman Empire.

Mehmet has gone down in history as one of the greatest conquerors the world has ever known. Today, more than five hundred years later, he is known as Mehmet Fatih, Mehmet the Conqueror, although he himself preferred the title "Avni", the "Helper," as he would like to have been remembered for his cultural and social achievements as well. As a wise ruler, he understood deeply the true meaning of the word "tolerance", allowing freedom of worship and freedom for each community to follow its own laws.

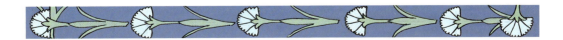

MEHMET THE CONQUEROR

1432:	Birth of Mehmet the Conqueror.
1451:	Mehmet succeeds to the throne.
1453:	Fall of Constantinople.
1455-1456:	Mehmet conquers Serbia and Bosnia.
1456:	Mehmet besieges Belgrade but fails to conquer it.
1458-1460:	Mehmet conquers most of present-day Greece.
1459:	Topkapi Palace started.
1461:	Mehmet conquers Albania.
1475:	Mehmet conquers the Crimea.
1478:	Topkapi Palace finished.
1480:	Mehmet besieges Rhodes but fails to conquer it.
1481:	Death of Mehmet the Conqueror.

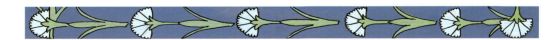

HEROES FROM THE EAST

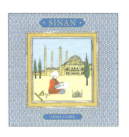

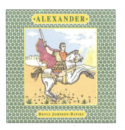
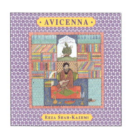

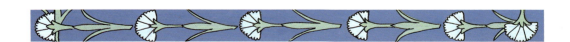